"Winshen Liu's *Paper Money* begins with 'Conjugation,' a poem that inventively enacts the slipperiness of language, especially for those immigrants who must negotiate a relationship with a new tongue, and therefore a new system of meaning. 'Catch // the rise before it falls to rose, lilac / to lily, orchid to orchard. Tell me / where we missed: strike // one, strike two, the clock strikes / twelve, the mouse runs down, and you're out / now sick, stricken, stroke.' It is a destabilizing and exhilarating ride. Other poems echo a legacy of poverty and ingenuity, in equal measure. It is food that provides the fundamental bond to family and cultural memory, in which Taiwan arrives in the steam of jasmine rice, a fig in the 'fancy food store' gives birth to yearning and to rhyme, and the 'nectared geyser' of white peaches becomes the nexus of elegiac pleasure. These poems awaken our own yearning for the universe of the senses that Liu renders with an exquisitely refined depth of observation. Tadpoles in a stream are 'jellied rain.' The throats of frogs are 'engorged / with the unsaid.' As the sensuous present tense meets up with the eternity of the dead, the ashes of the body become 'front teeth and fresh / paint, magician's wave and cuff links.' The impact of the whole is one in which the elegance of craft provides compressed containers for histories and feelings that would otherwise be unmanageable in their immensity, a treasure in paper money always on the verge of going up in smoke."

— Diane Seuss,
author of *frank: sonnets* and *Modern Poetry*

"Winshen Liu's poems examine peaches for ripeness and, with the magic only the best writers can conjure, finds a way to measure our own grief, hunger, poverty, and desire. These poems are a balm for anyone with an achy heart or an empty wallet. Winshen Liu is a staggering writer."

— José Olivarez,
author of *Promises of Gold*

"Elegant while elegiac, delicate and brimming with delicacies of image, Winshen Liu's *Paper Money* refuses to brittle where the feeling heart is most tempted to break. Every detail is precise like the arrangement of flowers, is considerate, is resonant with reverence and the aches of understanding. This work adeptly reveals the distances even love cannot completely close by trying to travel the distances only love can see. If money burns a hole in your pocket, spend it on this; send a poem up the sky to someone who needs a reminder that they're remembered, still."

— Cortney Lamar Charleston,
author of *Doppelganghanger*

"Despite their weighty subjects—poverty, migration and its attendant losses, familial love, grief—the poems in *Paper Money* feel mobile and vibrant as butterflies, set aloft by the freshness of Liu's voice and the light touch of her lines. The playful charm and delicate textures of these poems belie a profound depth of feeling, like handmade lace draped over an insistent, pulsing heart."

— Melissa Ginsburg,
author of *Dear Weather Ghost* and *Doll Apollo*

PAPER
MONEY

Winshen Liu

DRIFTWOOD
PRESS

Independently published by *Driftwood Press*
in the United States of America.

Managing Poetry Editor: Sara Moore Wagner
Guest Judge: Diane Seuss
Front & Back Cover Image: Ío Wuerich
Cover Design: Sally Franckowiak, James McNulty,
& Winshen Liu
Interior Design: James McNulty
Fonts: Rift Soft, Garamond, & Merriweather

First published on August 5, 2025
ISBN-13: 978-1-949065-37-4

Please visit our website at www.driftwoodpress.com
or email us at editor@driftwoodpress.net.

CONTENTS

Conjugation   1

inheritance   2

my friend posts a photo of her weekend
and i have the same memory   3

自強號 (zì qiáng hào)   4

White Peaches   5

Lunch at a tavern   6

Lunch Break   7

The Poor Man's Tax   8

After certain phone calls   9

Summer nights   10

The day before   17

Funerary Rites   18

樹葬 (shù zàng)   19

Cold, Hard Cash   20

Nostalgia   22

Lento Notes   23

Late Hydrangea   24

Can you love someone if
you don't know their birthday   25

August Peaches   27

Interview:
Starting with Two Suitcases   29

Conjugation

Be sure to pick the lime
before it ripens into lemon. Catch

the rise before it falls to rose, lilac
to lily, orchid to orchard. Tell me
where we missed: strike

one, strike two, the clock strikes
twelve, the mouse runs down, and you're out
now sick, stricken, stroke.

As in stroke of luck. Or genius. Light
strokes, smooth strokes. Oar
or brush, breast or butterfly.

Stroke a cat and flutter
past the boat house.

inheritance

> "...in my house, vaporub is for headaches,
> sore muscles, nightmares, & everything else."
>
> —José Olivarez, "Note: Vaporub"

the label was always rubbed off. in pockets and purses,
thumb-sized nesting dolls hid nubs the children found
by smell. mentholated trails like winter sweat.
           this mint stub

came from strip mall oriental marts and ran
across foreheads, into temples, under nostrils, until
it ran out and the father ran back for more. 薄荷
               chased after sighs

and closed eyes. it knocked when the house grew
hungry, the phone card, parched. when they sat
on the thirdhand couch, each wearing four coats,
                 when they slept

the same way and had to get up. it followed
the father up smokestacks, his fear of heights
falling like seasoning over tv dinners as
                   wheel of fortune

spun. the kids grew up, the marts closed down, phones froze
faces as voices. they learned to stuff pockets with lottery tickets,
but even with all their good english, the kids could never
                     solve the puzzle.

my friend posts a photo of her weekend and i have the same memory

from here, the sky is a glass of water, stitched
along its rim with late summer oaks. her son stands

half a thumbnail tall. head of black hair angled up,
arms out from his sides, his hands starred in wonder.

his dad arcs an arm toward the sky, pinning string
between his fingers as the invisible unspools. the same wind

floated my grandfather's laugh, as the two of us, the only ones
on the field, tugged a flying fish across the upturned lake.

自強號 (zì qiáng hào)

I heated leftovers for lunch today.

The lid sweat
as Taiwan arrived
in steam: jasmine
rice that had slept with a braised
egg, cabbage and carrots
stirred from a nap.

The office courtyard steeped
in the high light of a young sun,
one that had not yet seen the western
window of a southbound train, where
an aproned woman pushes
a cart of warm boxes car to car, asking
if you need one in song.

White Peaches

For you, that week, we bought peaches like eggs:
twelve in a box, more than we'd had in years:

pink-skinned and white-fleshed, portrait of Yang Guifei
in the morning, supple and unblemished:

the fridge became a vault that only
the right aunt, at the right hour, could open:

she sliced a wedge into tiny dice, rolled
into your bowl, no longer ceramic:

we watched them tremble and brown on your fork
and relearned what it meant to be eager;

the dilemma arose when four remained:
six weeks had passed and so they wrinkled:

we each touched the peaches: but no
one was hungry, not even at dinner.

Lunch at a tavern

The office courtyard has four tables, each
with four chairs. My coworkers sit

one person per table.
I think of the time my

mother and I shared a reuben,
the angular taste of rye bread.

She asked what my greatest fear was.
Roaches, heights, meaninglessness.

I bit into a fry and said spiders. She stared
behind me, at the diner by the blinds,

and said hers was eating alone.

Lunch Break

I roam the aisles at the fancy food store,
through isles of citrus and berries and grapes,
my mouth a desert, desirous of shapes
like whispered kisses to one I adore.

The fig displays, overflowing, arrest
my gaze: I freeze while my eyelashes paint
in air a still life impression, a faint
maroon beneath the green, Mission, Celeste.

The painting dries and my gaze is released.
I pick one up and behold its wee cheek.
A pinch, a squeeze, how I'd love to just sneak
a palmful home as a poor woman's feast.

The Poor Man's Tax

My aunts call and ask me to buy
twenty tickets this time. They will pay
me back, they assure and assure me,
even though I have bought them and do not ask.

They conjure the years my father drove
to the store, a not-on-the-way stop
on our way home, spending one-dollar
gas to buy two-dollar paper, how all I saw

was an augury of loss.
The weekly drop
into state coffers.
These slips, stacked
into a hand, grow warm now,
between my palms for hours.

After certain phone calls

At the seventh hour, watch
for tadpoles. They race
in heats, one cloud
after the other, down
the once-dry creek
bed, streaking it with
their jellied rain. This
swimming swells their twin origins
into frogs, with bulbous
throats, those muscled balloons, pronounced.

Feel the membrane stretched across the soft,
white drums, engorged
with the unsaid. See
how the wet fibers hold, taut like globe grapes,
peeled, but still intact.

Summer Nights

Tuesday night

climbs

into bed

as   a   chorus   of   cricket   chirps   in

your   breath

moonlight

greases

your hair

a 手抓餅

left on

the frying pan

your limbs

in angles   I envy

over   and   over

                              I   close

          my   eyes

                    will

that   steady

          rise   and   fall

                    measure   for   measure   line

                    after   line

                    but the refrain
          refrains

from   opening

outside

        the   streets   are   bright

            enough to   read
                        while walking

steel-glass stories
               pull

       my   unwilling   irises

                      up

                   echo

your star-cued

      crickets

I   thumb   through

avenue   after

avenue   looking

for   one   with   lullaby

lights

my   eyes
grow

stale   my   fingertips
peel

my ears   will   split

for silence

block   by

block

    I   roam

then

between

volumes

the light

tips

and   I

arrive

back

to   you   closer   to

morning

than night

The day before

We mist gifted orchids
and pluck anthers off lilies.

I find the water in my throat
to ask my near-sighted cousins
what they will wear tomorrow.

It feels important to know how to cry
with glasses on.

Funerary Rites

I have only been to funerals for grandfathers.

Twenty years passed between one and the next, so I
       forgot what to expect.

The internet was right: there are one hundred days of
       mourning and the men do not shave.

"Loud crying is a common practice at Chinese funerals."
       As if there is a dial.

As if everyone else studies quiet crying in a basement on
       Wednesday nights.

The internet was wrong. There was only the sound of
       fuzzy fingers knotting tissue threads.

樹葬 (shù zàng)

You always flossed and wore collared shirts.

Did you know the ash would be white?

I expected the gray of attic labels and alley cats,

that the urn would open and pour out

the earth like shavings —

                              but it was lustrous.

Burned into stardust, sun sand and

moon banks, front teeth and fresh

paint, magician's wave and cuff links.

                    I will burn paper money for you.

Cold, Hard Cash
after Tina Chang

It is the hour of dew. The sparrows tune
their voices to the pitch of suburban lawns. Always
that same thread of copper circles, pockets of square air lying
at your center, a marble deity watching

over you. My father thinks you are powerful
as he whispers your praises, images of gold
spheres, solid and growing.
I think of your dried scales rusting.

You once slept in an unborn tunnel, your skeleton pressed
from stars. Cropped meteors stabbed
the air when you were caught,
the stone and soil baking. Drills carved

the whole of you, the bit spinning so furiously,
it could smoke as you broke off from land.
An inverted mausoleum, a terraced pit,
dug to disinter you. I know how much has been seized:

the leaching and electrowinning, the faith
in your forebears yielding rice
in a bowl, your raw angles pounded smooth.
The sulphuric poison is real.

The deaths of little egrets and masked palm civets
can be found by smelling palms
that covet warmed coins. The crumble of the earth
and all its verdant life, amphibians, winged bodies

can be felt in one clench. And so my father bows
three times, then prostrates. As he mutters, he prays
for you with hands that open and close, paper to ore;
you lay mute on this bare

altar even when he stands. This daily tightening
of your sheened grip, your engraved face
again imprints onto his eyes and lips,
too devoted to ever defeat you.

Nostalgia

In Taitung, we
used to twist
a metal daisy
then push a gold
leaf until the *ts-ts*
ignited the blue
goblin. I worried
either I or the house
would explode:
my cousin and I
would die, naked,
save for the shower
caps and slippers
our grandparents kept
from their hotel
stay in Taipei.
The pink plastic
mugs we clutched
to ladle bath
water would loll
about the drain.
Now, hot water
comes fumeless,
without ado. Mugs
hung just to brush teeth.
Sometimes, while sudsing
my hair into wet cotton,
I listen for the flicker.

Lento Notes

I burn my tongue on a scallion

pancake and grief makes me take a second

bite. But grief is not the canyon, glowing

like the inside of a persimmon pressed

open by thumbs; it is all of the hours,

and only ever those hours, waiting

for that glow. At the end of autumn, it sheds

the lento notes of a nocturne you've never

heard, that I wanted to play over

the phone but didn't, for fear

it would not sound as sweet

on the pentatonic scale.

Late Hydrangea

each day opens with her
index grazing the periwinkle
dome. suspended whimsical
lattice.

the blossom meets its end
long before it papers
the table. every pistil still
intact.

at the dawn of limp tuft
or freckled leaf, she pinches
a plush of petals: the whole
piece, binned.

she insists on knowing
this singular form, shuns
more mourning
indoors.

Can you love someone if
you don't know their birthday

My grandfather only ever called us
by our nicknames. My cousins
were Autumn Sky and Magnesium
Beauty. I was Warmth of the Morning Sun.

We knew not to play during the news
and his naps, but in the small window
when we could bumble sol-mi-mi's, did we
echo our mothers, on the same out-of-tune keys?

One night, as our family clinked East Wind
against Fortune, he surprised us with forbidden
treats at a forbidden hour: a dozen streetcorner baos.
One per person, except, counting now, we were thirteen—

I can still hear the gulp of his glasses
case closing and his Sichuan curl
when he gave his catchphrase.

"It's okay" is what I say to my dog
when she barks at the keys charging
back to their locks down the hall.

August Peaches

We must eat the peaches today
for they are about to burst.

We left them like still
art until they softened
our longing
and stored each sunset.
But now, it is late
summer and no one
else is coming to visit.

In our palms, they crump
into twice-sliced
stars, pressed in
on the edges, sluicing
blushed juice. One brush
with water might bruise
its furred flesh,
we might dive
to kiss the counter, lick
the lines on our fingers,
and suck and suck
every ounce oozed
out. The first bite
will set off
its nectared geyser—
bright and quick,
tartsweet meteor,
chasing the inch
of our chins
our tongues cannot reach.

STARTING WITH TWO SUITCASES
A Conversation with
Winshen Liu & Sara Moore Wagner

First, congratulations on winning the 2024 Adrift Chapbook contest, judged by Diane Seuss! Your manuscript was also a favorite of mine and other editors at *Driftwood*. We're so honored to have you join our catalogue. We were all drawn into how much you say in such small spaces with your exacting language and images. Tell us about your journey as a poet!

Thank you so much, Sara! I was so excited to receive this news and am honored to be published with *Driftwood*. Thank you to Diane Seuss and everyone at *Driftwood* for bringing *Paper Money* out in the world. I hadn't at all been part of the poetry world and still feel like "poet" is a title I have yet to earn. I'm working on it, though!

I imagine I'm like most contemporary poets in that I didn't expect to be a poet. Growing up, I loved my English classes, but not poetry. I liked novels. I started college intending to be an English major, but the syllabi for the required lit courses scared me. I couldn't believe they assigned a book a week. Back then I had never read so quickly and didn't think I could manage something like *Anna Karenina* at that pace, so I opted to take two poetry courses instead. I thought I was outsmarting the system and saving myself some time, but I ended up needing just as much if not more time understanding poems! After those classes, I didn't read or write any poetry. I switched majors and managed to graduate with a focus on race and East Asians in Latin America.

Afterwards, I spent a year in China on a research fellowship before realizing academia wasn't for me. I worked at a tech startup for a few years then went back to school for computer science (I was curious what it was all about.) In 2021, I left tech to write a novel and worked in food service and retail. Poetry still wasn't on my mind at all. One of my jobs was at a bookstore, and I remember saying things like, "No one reads poetry."

But after a year, my novel wasn't ready and I needed a more stable desk job. I was hoping to not return to tech, so I found a role at The Poetry Foundation and that changed my whole trajectory. I had no idea what *Poetry* magazine was, but suddenly, I was learning how vibrant the contemporary poetry world was. Every morning (to catch up, if you will), I read poems and that prompted me to write them. I was very lucky to have a few friends read some and encourage me to keep writing, and soon, I realized so much of what I had been writing in fiction had failed because those stories were meant to be poems. A year later, I started my MFA in poetry at the University of Mississippi. About half of these poems were written in my first semester, so I feel very lucky to have had this opportunity to write and be with other writers.

This is an astonishing journey, and it shows how divergent roads can lead, eventually, to something like a "true calling." I personally think this kind of journey, gathering experience beyond school before settling into writing, makes for better poetry. What is your take on how these experiences, in addition to the reading you did at *Poetry*, have shaped your poetry? Does your experience in the tech world inform how you craft a poem at all?

Time has helped me arrive at writing, but I think the tech route was more of a necessary one without much influence (as far as I can tell) on what I'm writing. It has meant I am able to write, because I was able to save money and have health insurance.

Writing was something I loved as a kid, but it wasn't something I actively thought about or wanted to do; I took up creative writing when we moved to New York City as a way to make friends outside of work. The writing class helped with that, and I'm lucky to still be in touch with friends from that class five years later, but during the eight-week course, I realized how alive I felt and how much I wanted to keep writing. Clichés, I know, but they did set me on a different path.

I am sure there would be wonderful ways to incorporate elements of computer science in my writing, but I think coding feels more like a job to me, so it hasn't been an influence or something I've wanted to bring into my writing. I did love proofs and algorithms, though, and I like puzzles and strategy board games, so maybe after I've been writing poetry for a long time, and after distancing myself from the job/paycheck aspects of tech for a longer period of time, I will find the play and joy in fusing my poems with some code.

I'd love to hear about your poetic influences for this book. Do you see *Paper Money* fitting into a lineage of books, in any way? Were there books you read to help you shape this collection that you'd like to recommend?

One of the things I love about poetry is how much each poem and book feel like they are part of a conversation and community, more so than novels. I love other forms, but I feel clearer resonances between poems, maybe because so much has been stripped away. Many of the earliest poetry books I read spurred me to write, and I think they very much shaped not only the poems in *Paper Money* but also my poetics. I hope *Paper Money* shows a connection to works like *Book of My Nights* by Li-Young Lee, *Half-Lit Houses* by Tina Chang, *OBIT* by Victoria Chang, and *Citizen Illegal* by José Olivarez. I recently re-read these and can still say I highly recommend all of them.

Paper Money is centered on the experience of immigration across generations. How close is this to your own family's story? Is there any background information you'd like to share with our audience?

I wrote these poems without a specific project in mind, but I suppose it's only natural that they converged around immigration and family. I don't have anything specific to share other than that my parents immigrated from Taiwan to the US at a time when the American Dream was maybe more alive for them than I see it now. So many of these poems were concerned with money, isolation, and nostalgia (nostalgia in its purest form, the pain of missing home as opposed to a longing for bygone times), and the persistence of those feelings as the child of immigrants. I also think the core of these poems is loss of a loved one, as informed by this immigration. What do love and grief look like for someone you haven't spent much time with? When there are maybe a handful of memories, and more years of distance than proximity?

Can you tell us a little more about the evolution of the American Dream since the days your parents immigrated? How has your opinion changed over time?

We should get dinner some time and chat on this! This is

a huge question and I'm sure it merits much more than what I'll share here. As a start, I consider the American Dream to be a rags-to-riches story, based on meritocracy, where anyone can arrive in America and "make it." I think it was easy for me to latch onto this idea, seeing as my parents came here for their graduate degrees. So even though they came from the poorest county in Taiwan, they immigrated as part of a privileged class. There are ways both their stories and mine are easy to narrate as exactly that: the American Dream. Starting with two suitcases and ending with a house and car, thanks to hard work and a good education.

College started challenging my ideas on this, mostly through readings and conversations, and years later, when I was working, I came to doubt that anything like the American Dream could exist in our country. It's the exception that wins and is held up as the rule, when the masses are telling a different story. Anand Giridharadas's *Winners Take All* applied a lot of the social theory I was supposed to have learned in college to the tech industry and did the greatest work in shifting my paradigm on tech, philanthropy, and, ultimately, the American Dream. I see this narrative as not only untrue, but a lot more nefarious now. I don't think my parents see it that way; they are maybe closer to the parents depicted in Ayad Akhtar's *Homeland Elegies*, where there is a sense of pride and gratitude towards this country because of their experience of the "American Dream."

One of other things I love about *Paper Money* is the way you use food. There isn't enough food in poems, and I really enjoy the experience of food as an image. I'm thinking about poets like Aimee Nezhukumatathil who do this to highlight cultural differences in a sensory way. This feels true here, too, especially in poems like "Lunch at a tavern," which highlights the disconnect between Eastern and Western culture. How and why you use food as a connecting image here. Is it a natural impulse or something planned?

It is natural. It's also unexpected. I usually have an emotion I am trying to linger with/in, and I think food ends up being my instinctive vehicle for it. Of course there are some poems, like "自強號 (zì qiáng hào)" and "August Peaches," where I'm prompted by a specific food and from there, I arrive at a thought or emotion. But generally, I think I arrive at the page without any food in mind. It appears of its own volition! For instance, with "White Peaches," I was very much focused on my grandfather near the end of his life when I wrote this and white peaches happened to carry the care and love we felt for him.

I love that you offered this understanding of "Lunch at a tavern," because it reminds me of how this poem started. (This was one of the first poems I wrote as an adult, and my subsequent returns to it have been more focused on the speaker living the mother's fear.) I think people sitting alone to eat is a very American thing and an example of how certain spaces or situations create the feeling of aloneness. In contrast, I think it is common (though maybe this is fading with the rise in privatization, inequality, and globalization) outside the US to share tables at restaurants. It feels like such a telling image of the American value for the individual versus cultures that value the communal.

I am really drawn to your use of the colon throughout the collection. At times it's a transition or doorway, other times, an emphasis or comparison. What do you love about a colon? When do you think is the best time to use one?

Thank you! I love this question, but I don't have deep thoughts on using colons beyond in "White Peaches." In that poem, I liked how flexible colons were. They can do all the things you mentioned, and I especially leaned on it to create a sense of prolonging. With someone nearing their end of life, there are complicated feelings of wanting them to be free of their suffering but also of wanting, always, more time together. The colon, I think, let me convey this dichotomy and introduce a special space in the poem, where each colon is like a "carried comma." This is just a term I'm making up, so what I mean is, if a comma is normally like a pause, the colon is like a pause while holding your hand. You're carried in that pause, because something more expansive will come after or a whole new space will be opened whereas the comma is for a more straightforward continuation or an aside.

I love the idea of the "carried comma!" That could be an essay in itself! This book includes some Chinese characters, words like "Mint" are written out this way. What was behind your choice to include these?

Thank you for this question! I think there's so much to discuss here and I am always curious how writers include multiple languages in their work. For these poems, the Chinese characters are for words I cannot translate into English and ones I think are a little present, like a wink or nod of IYKYK to readers who speak Mandarin or are Taiwanese American like me. For instance, with the mint in "inheritance" as you mentioned, I am referencing a very specific item that is called "mint" in Chinese, even though it is a ChapStick-shaped product that looks almost like hard candy, translucent and scented strongly with mint. People rub this on their temples to ease headaches. I grew up around a lot of it, but I have no idea what it is really called, or how I would really translate it, so I went with the Chinese characters to keep that item intact. I am trying to both write in English but not cater to the white gaze and English-only audience, so I aimed to write a poem that made sense even without knowing what 薄荷 is. I also think it's okay if a reader is confused by or bothered by not knowing what these characters say. Of course, for readers who can read Mandarin and English, the poem may feel ever so slightly clearer, and for specifically Taiwanese American readers, my hope is that preserving this word in Mandarin creates another plane in the poem. We can meet and interact there because of our shared understanding of 薄荷.

Similarly, "自強號 (zì qiáng hào)" and "樹葬 (shù zàng)" are words that said exactly what I meant. I did not have another way to title those poems. But I thought it would be too alienating for a reader to not be able to reference a poem, simply because they could not pronounce the title. It doesn't bother me if people read a poem and have to skip over words from another language, but I still want each poem to be approachable, so I added the hanyu pinyin for those two poems, just in their titles. This way, people can at least pronounce the titles in conversation.

One last consideration is that we live in a society where people can look up these characters if they really want to. I know not everyone has access to the internet and smartphones that can translate images, but I think the vast majority of people can do this, so if they really, really want to know what a Chinese character says, they can. I think by keeping the characters and not translating them, it's an invitation to do this!

Absolutely. I love that! As someone who doesn't speak Mandarin, I found it easy to look up things I didn't understand. Even skipping over words, the poems are so rich. It's absolutely accurate they aren't, as you said, catering to that "white gaze." Do you have any advice for other poets who are hoping to enter the space of language interrogation while writing primarily in English? Is there anything you made sure to avoid doing?

I'm glad! That's so good to hear, and I'm glad I'm not the only one who looks up words when reading poems with other languages in them. Ease of translation is one benefit of the tech we have now! I didn't want to italicize words in other languages or translate when it felt like the translation would lose so much. I don't have advice, per se, but when I'm writing, I do think of the tech concept of "Easter eggs," where a gift is hidden for those who can find it. If you happen to know a few words in Mandarin or have the means to look it up, you find the egg and can access a certain delight contained in it. And if you don't, that's okay. That may be a silly analogy, but it captures some of how I think of cultural references and words in other languages while writing in English.

I want to talk about the title, which references the lottery tickets your aunts yearn for, poverty and the way the American government preys on hopeful poor, and your funerary rites for your grandfather. Can you tell us more about "paper money" as an idea, and the burning of it as ritual? In a way, "paper money" seems more sacred than the "Cold Hard Cash," which feels menacing!

Yes, absolutely. I liked the multiple meanings "paper money" offered. First and foremost for me, paper money is literally a sacred thing. Joss paper is used in folk religions and Buddhism in Taiwan, and fire is used to transport things from this world to the afterlife, so burning joss paper for someone gives them money in the afterlife. I very much wanted to draw on this, and the title came to me from one of the first poems I wrote, "樹葬 (shù zàng)," where, at the burial, the speaker says, "I will burn paper money for you." I wanted this chapbook to honor this tradition, pay my respects, and express how much I love and miss people who have passed on.

Of course, "paper money" means something completely different in America, and I really liked how this term could bring in almost an opposite set of meanings, closer to "play money" in a board game. I thought this captured some of what it can feel like for immigrants, arriving with very little money in such a consumerist country. Even after finding one's footing, America has such high income inequality. I wanted to comment on the feeling of having money but never enough of it and how money is really nothing of substance. This thing called money, that we work for and fight over, is made up. It's just paper, or sometimes not even as physical as paper. It's numbers on a screen and I thought "paper money" poked fun at this, like a dig at something considered so precious, especially when money, as the key instrument facilitating capitalism, ends up doing so much harm.

At the center of this book is grief, grief for that "American Dream," but more specifically for the grandfather. The poet Erica Jong said, "All poetry from the beginning is about Eros and Thanatos." Grief combines love and death. How did you go about approaching a topic so vast and difficult? Do you have any favorite poems or collections about grief?

Thank you for sharing Jong's words with me. I don't know of her work, but I would love to read more. I agree very much with her statement, how the act of death sets off an unending love for the person who has died. I think Victoria Chang's and Li-Young Lee's works were instrumental for getting me to write about grief. The first poems I wrote responded simply to city scenes and I might have continued on that path, but with the timing of events and because I came across their books, I saw what could happen on the page. Chang's work was an example for a free virtual poetry class. A friend of a friend was teaching, so I signed up and the first work we looked at was a selection from *OBIT*. It resonated and inspired me, and at some point, while working at The Poetry Foundation, I think I came across Lee and thought *Book of My Nights* is such a beautiful title. I started reading from there.

Having read (and written!) some more since then, a few of my favorite collections on grief include: *Against Heaven* by Kemi Alabi, *Your Emergency Contact Has Experienced an Emergency* by Chen Chen, *Ghost Of* by Diana Khoi Nguyen, *Silent Anatomies* by Monica Ong, and *I'm Always So Serious* by Karisma Price.

What's next for you?

I have very little idea, but I will hopefully get to continue writing and be with other writers!

Thank you, dear reader, for picking up this book. It's a gift to have these poems in your hands and I'm grateful to every person who reads poetry, let alone mine. I'm grateful to editors and readers of literary magazines for their hard work keeping poetry alive and well. (A special thanks to those who published early versions of poems in this chapbook, including Barbara Westwood Diehl at *Baltimore Review*, Hannah Bonner at *BRINK*, and Cortney Lamar Charleston while at *The Rumpus*.) Thank you, Diane Seuss, for reading my work and choosing this chapbook out of so many great manuscripts. I am deeply honored and grateful, for your selection and for the confidence you have given me to continue on with poetry. Thank you to Sara Moore Wagner and James McNulty at *Driftwood Press* for your enthusiasm and care since day one of working together. I am so lucky to have my first chapbook out with such a wonderful press. I would not have submitted my chapbook had it not been for the de Groot Foundation. Thank you for supporting my poetry and helping me get it out into the world. It is hard emotionally and financially to get poems published, so thank you, Charles and Clydette, for changing this reality into one of optimism and possibility for so many writers. Thank you to Holly Amos, Angela Flores, Lindsay Garbutt, Hannah Kucharzak, Juj Lepe, Adrian Matejka, Jake Skeets, and my workshop-mates for reading some of the earliest drafts of many of these poems and supporting me in my first year in an MFA program. Thank you to Beth Ann Fennelly, Melissa Ginsburg, Derrick Harriell, and Aimee Nezhukumatathil for seeing potential in my early poetry and being such generous, thoughtful teachers. I am so grateful to have gotten to learn from you. Al Favilla, Stefania Gomez, and Lisa Low, thank you for being my star poetry friends. I look up to you, I adore you and your work, and I am so grateful for your friendship. I cannot wait til your collections are out! Thank you to Jillian Elkin, Claudia Hinz, and Michael Falcone, my dear prose friends who graciously read my poems and offered some of the greatest encouragement I've needed on this writing journey. A heartfelt thanks to Dawnie Walton, for being my writing mentor, for believing in me all these years (even if poetry isn't really her thing), and helping me stay on this path. Thank you for your brilliance, kindness, and support. And the greatest of thanks to my husband, to my parents, grandparents, and aunts who are like second mothers to me—I wish your sacrifices didn't need to be. I love you endlessly. These poems are for you.

Winshen Liu's poetry has appeared in *Cincinnati Review, Electric Literature, The Malahat Review,* and *The Rumpus,* among others. She is grateful to the University of Mississippi faculty for their mentorship and the de Groot Foundation for supporting her work. In addition to writing, she loves long-distance train travel, baking and bakeries, and stickers. You can follow her work at winshenliu.com.

"自強號 (zì qiáng hào)" *Baltimore Review,* 2022
"White Peaches" *Bellevue Literary Review,* 2024
"Funerary Rites" *Brink,* 2023
"Lunch Break" *Cincinnati Review,* 2023
"After certain phone calls" *december,* 2023
"Vegetarian Instant Ramen" *Grist,* 2025
"Nostalgia" *The Malahat Review,* 2023
"Lunch at a tavern" *Ninth Letter,* 2023
"The day before" *RHINO,* 2023
"樹葬 (shù zàng)" and "Lento Notes" *The Rumpus,* 2023
"inheritance" *Variant Lit,* 2024

OTHER
DRIFTWOOD PRESS
TITLES

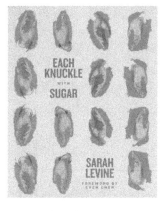